SpringerBriefs in Educational and Technology

More information about this series at http://www.springer.com/series/11821

Joseph Frantiska, Jr.

Visualization Tools for Learning Environment Development

 Springer

Joseph Frantiska, Jr.
Contributing Faculty Member
Walden University
Minneapolis, MN, USA

ISSN 2196-498X   ISSN 2196-4998   (electronic)
SpringerBriefs in Educational Communications and Technology
ISBN 978-3-319-67439-1   ISBN 978-3-319-67440-7   (eBook)
https://doi.org/10.1007/978-3-319-67440-7

Library of Congress Control Number: 2017953950

This Springer imprint is published by Springer Nature
The registered company is Springer International Publishing AG
The registered company address is: Gewerbestrasse 11, 6330 Cham, Switzerland

This brief is dedicated to my mother Madeline and to my late father Joseph Sr.

Techniques and Tools of Visualization

A carpenter uses tools such as hammers and saws along with building techniques like measuring and framing. When developing a learning environment, there is a need for tools and techniques as well. Just as the carpenter uses them to create a functional and esthetic structure, the developer of a learning environment utilizes them to develop a functional and user-friendly environment. In this brief, we will discuss various tools and techniques to create learning environments.

Preface

Software and systems engineers have for years used various tools that allow them to understand and visualize a project prior to completion and release to the user community. As educators continue to develop their own software projects, they also have a need to visualize the operations of their software prior to usage by their students or other practitioners.

In Chap. 1, the background and history of visualization tools are discussed along with their importance to the engineering profession and how this translates to the educator/developer. Chapter 2 examines the utility and development of use case diagrams and how they allow the visualization of the functionality of the system. Chapter 3 describes the usage of the IPO (Input-Processing-Output) diagram. The IPO diagram as its name implies allows the visualization of the information flow through the software. Specifically, what are the required inputs, how are they used or processed, and what are the required outputs. Chapter 4 discusses the implementation of flowcharts. While IPO diagrams represent the information flow, flowcharts delineate the detailed processing of the information. That is, flowcharts are a more detailed implementation of the processing portion of IPO diagrams. The subject of Chap. 5 is the entity-relationship diagram (ERD). Chapter 6 discusses the more in-depth technical standards for learning objects.

It is the goal of this brief to aid the educator in visualizing their software projects both internally and externally. In this way, they can create learning environments efficiently so that their productivity is optimized and in turn so will be the learning of their students.

Joseph Frantiska, Jr.

Contents

Background and Significance

As educators become more adept at using technology, they have the power to develop more sophisticated learning objects such as multimedia, websites, and animations. Just like their software developer counterparts, they have a need to visualize their applications throughout the design and development processes.

The dictionary defines visualization as the act of forming a mental image of something. The visualization of a common object or process such as a ball or mailing a letter is relatively easy. However, how can someone visualize the behavior (internal or external) of a software application even before it exists?

For the application developer, the ability to understand the applications' performance and behavior is imperative so that they provide the required result. Flowcharting can provide this insight.

The applicability of flowcharting to a wide range of applications developed by people with a wide range of technical ability allows for the understanding of the complexity. It also provides a means to describe and verify the application's arcane aspects such as construction and usage to people without this intimate knowledge in a succinct, logical method. It is the map to be followed, the narration that articulates the story (Frantiska 2009).

Industrial engineer Frank Gilbreth, known as the father of time and motion studies, was in his unending quest to find out the most efficient means to perform various tasks when he developed the flow process chart. He introduced this first structured method for documenting process flow to members of the American Society of Mechanical Engineers (ASME) in 1921 in the presentation titled "Process Charts – First Steps in Finding the One Best Way".

Gilbreth developed this and other tools which quickly became adopted into industrial engineering curricula. The early 1930s saw another industrial engineer, Allan H. Mogensen, who began training sessions in the use of some industrial engineering tools at his Work Simplification Conferences in Lake Placid, New York, over the next fifty years as a result of embracing Gilbreth's ideas.

One attendee of a 1944 Mogensen class was Arthur Spinanger, who would become the head of Procter and Gamble's industrial engineering department where he developed their Deliberate Methods Change Program. Another 1944 graduate was Benjamin S. Graham of Standard Register Corporation, where he adapted the flow process chart used to improve factory work to streamline information processing. He developed the multiflow process chart which enabled the display of multiple documents and their relationships.

In 1947, ASME adopted a standardized set of symbols derived from Gilbreth's original work which they called the Standard for Process Charts. Moving from the factory floor to information processing and then to the computer age, mathematician Herman Goldstine developed flowcharts with fellow mathematician and computing pioneer John von Neumann at Princeton University to aid in the development of early electronic computers.

Reference

Frantiska, J. (2009). Knowing the flow: How flowcharting can help visualize software application development. *ISTE Journal for Computing Teachers-Online*, Spring.

Chapter 1
Use Case Diagrams

One technique widely used to create various types of systems such as a learning environment is the use case. This is a technique used to describe a system's behavior as it responds to a request or stimulus from outside of the system. A use case describes "who" can do "what" with the system in question. The use case technique is used to capture a system's behavior by specifying functionality based upon various scenarios that the system may be required to experience.

Scope and Goals of a Use Case

A particular use case contains single or multiple scenarios that dictate how a system will interface with individuals or other systems dependent upon a specific objective. Instead of highly arcane technical language, they use terms which are familiar to the individual or system that it is interacting with.

In 1986, Ivar Jacobson, an important contributor to the Unified Modeling Language (UML) and Unified Process, originated the concept of the use case. Jacobson's idea was influential and groundbreaking. Numerous contributions have been made to the subject since then but the most significant contributor has been American computer scientist Alistair Cockburn. His seminal 2000 book *Writing Effective Use Cases* laid down the framework of what use cases are and how they can be written in a structured and efficient manner.

Since the 1990s, use cases became one of the most common ways to understand or define the functionality of a system.

A use case describes a singular system behavior to accomplish a singular objective. Therefore, many use cases could be required to understand the set of behaviors that comprise a complete system.

Actors are external entities that interact with the system; an actor can be a user, a group of users based upon one or more characteristics, or other systems. A use

© Association for Educational Communications and Technology (AECT) 2018
J. Frantiska, Jr., *Visualization Tools for Learning Environment Development*,
SpringerBriefs in Educational Communications and Technology,
https://doi.org/10.1007/978-3-319-67440-7_1

case defines the interactions between actors and the system to accomplish a certain task. For example, a use case for an automated teller machine (ATM) might view the ATM as the system and the various customers as actors who will interact with the ATM to accomplish various tasks such as checking balances, making deposits, and making withdrawals. Depending on the task, the system will need to behave in a certain way. Also, another actor could be the bank that the ATM interacts with based upon its interactions with the customers (Cockburn 2000).

Use cases aren't concerned with what processes occur within system. They treat a system as a "black box" that is viewed only in terms of its inputs, outputs, and transfer characteristics without any knowledge of its internal workings. This is a deliberate practice, since it simplifies the description of requirements, and avoids the trap of making assumptions about how the internal functionality will be accomplished.

The Unified Modeling Language

Many people are exposed to the construct of the use case through the language that describes them. That language is Unified Modeling Language (UML) which provides a diagrammatical scheme for depicting use cases which is called the use case model. It is a common misunderstanding that UML defines the nature of what a use case is. However, UML's graphical notation can only give the most basic synopsis of a use case or related group of use cases.

The most important utility of a use case in creating a learning environment is twofold. First, the diagrammatical notation of a system's behavior is based on a learning objective. What is emphasized is the benefit delivered by the system to outside entities such as end users or other systems.

Second, the circumstance of the use case as a member of a set of use cases is stressed. A complete collection of uniform, succinct use cases gives a comprehensive understanding of the full system conduct. In turn, a common dialogue between the user and the creator of the system is provided.

Through the diagrammatical notation, use cases are depicted by ovals and the actors or entities interacting with the system are represented by simple stick figures. Using a university as a basis for use case development, the Student actor can perform various actions such as Enroll_Course, Attend_Course, or Pay_Bill while the Dean actor can Approve_Course. There are some use cases that involve multiple actors such as the Pay_Bill use case where both the Student and the Bursar are involved. The box bounds the University System so that the use cases are part of the system with the actors being excluded.

A use case diagram details the interactions between actors and the system but not between the actors themselves. If that actor to actor interaction is necessary for the understanding of how the system works, the interactions can be added and the boundaries of the use case need to be reconfigured if necessary. Interacting actors can be included within the suppositions that the use case is based on. End users whether they are human or systems can be represented by multiple actors since actors reflect an entities role within the system. For example, the Dean and the Faculty may be the same person.

There are three major relationships among use cases. First, a given use case may *include* another. The first use case can be dependent on the outcome of the use case included within it. This is useful for extracting truly common behaviors from several use cases into a single description.

Second, a given use case, (the extension) may *extend* another. This relationship indicates that the behavior of the extension use case may be inserted in the extended use case under some conditions. Its utility arises in working with special scenarios or in the incorporation of new requirements while a system is undergoing maintenance and extension.

Third, a relationship exists where a use case can be a generalized form of another use case. This parent – child relationship is useful in defining overlapping roles between actors (i.e. a dean of a college can also be a faculty member). A generalization relationship is when a specialized (child) element is based on a general (parent) element. While the parent model element can have one or more children, and any child model element can have one or more parents, typically a single parent has multiple children. Generalization relationships appear in class, component, and use case diagrams. Figure 1.1 details these relationships in the university example.

Appropriate Degree of Detail

Some projects require a relatively simple use case structure while other required a more complex structure. In general, the degree of complexity of the project has a direct correspondence to the required complexity and degree of detail of the use case(s).

In addition to the complexity of the project, the project's progress can impact the required level of detail in a use case. That is, the use case can be a function of time as well as project complexity. The use cases required at the beginning of a project may be brief. However, as the development progresses the required level of detail for use cases decreases. This reflects the different requirements of the use case. Initially they need only be brief because they are used to summarize the learning objective from the learner perspective. However, later in the process, designers need far more specific and detailed guidance.

There is no standard structure for detailed use cases. However, there exists agreement about the critical sections; for most use cases. The typical sections are follows:

Name
A use case name must be unique and describe the particular use case. It needs to be written in verb-noun format (e.g., *Select Color, Withdraw Tuition*), it describes an achievable objective (e.g., *Select Type* is better than *Selecting Type*) and allows the

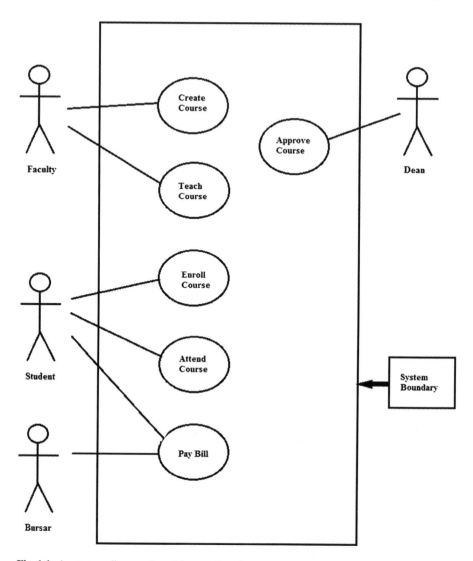

Fig. 1.1 A use case diagram describing a university

learner to understand what the use case describes. Names should two or three words long to describe the use case briefly but accurately.

Version

Since uses cases will change over time as the project changes, a version section describing the current section may be needed. When the project is just beginning, the use case that describes the high level may be different from the later use case when the software is being developed. Older versions of the use case may still be current documents, because they may be valuable to different types of designers.

Summary

A summary section is used to provide a concise overview when reading the longer, full description is unnecessary. An optimal summary is a few sentences or at most a paragraph and includes the goal and principal actor.

Actors

An actor is an entity outside the system that can be of two types: primary or secondary. A primary actor acts on the system while a secondary actor is acted upon by the system. An actor may be a person, a device, another system or sub-system, or time. Actors represent the different roles that something outside has in its relationship with the system whose functional requirements are being specified. For instance, within the context of the university example, actors can represent faculty members, students, administrative staff, the admissions system, and the tuition system. An individual in the real world can be represented by several actors if they have several different roles and goals regarding a system such as the faculty member who is also a dean and a researcher. These interact with system and do some action on that.

Preconditions

A *preconditions* section defines all preconditions that is, the conditions that must be true for the *trigger* (see below) to initiate the use case. For example, a use case for an automated teller machine simulator is called Withdraw Cash. A precondition for Withdraw Cash is that the customer has an ATM card with their bank account information that fits in the card reader, has a personal PIN number, and is registered with the bank as an ATM customer.

Triggers

A *trigger* is the event that causes the use case to be initiated. This event can be external such as user actions, temporal such as programs scheduled to run at certain times or internal such as a piece of software within the environment is run.

Basic Course of Events

Each use case should include a basic course of events, also called "basic flow". A basic course of events is often conveyed as a set of steps that are usually numbered. For example, with the aforementioned ATM: The ATM prompts the user to log on. The user inserts his card and enters his password. The system verifies the logon information, and if accepted, the system logs user on to the system.

Alternative Paths

Use cases may contain alternative paths or scenarios, which are variations on the basic flow. An alternate flow describes a scenario other than the basic flow that results in a user completing his or her goal. In the ATM example, the basic flow includes the user entering their valid password and then entering the system. An alternate flow would be if the password was found to be invalid and the system issues an error message prompting the user to enter a valid password.

Exceptions are procedures that are executed when things go wrong within the system. They may be described, not in the alternative paths section but in a section of their own. Alternative paths make use of the numbering of the basic course of events to show at which point they differ from the basic scenario, and, if appropriate, where they rejoin. The intention is to avoid repeating information unnecessarily.

An example of an alternative path would be: "The system recognizes cookie on user's machine", and "Go to step 4 (Main path)". An example of an exception path would be: "The system does not recognize user's logon information", and "Go to step 1 (Main path)"

Postconditions

The *post-conditions* section describes what the change in state of the system will be after the use case completes. Post-conditions are guaranteed to be true when the use case ends.

Business Rules

Business rules are written (or unwritten) rules or policies that determine how an organization conducts its business regarding a use case. They are requirements that represent constraints on system behaviors, rather than behaviors themselves.

Examples:

All transactions are in U.S. Dollars. (ATM example)

Valid operator's license is required to rent a car. (Rent-a-car example)

Late-fee is assessed for enrollment after the second week of the semester. (College enrollment example)

Notes

Regardless of how well designed a use case is, the designer will have some information that does not fit under a specific situation or exception. Well-designed use cases will include a section (e.g. "Notes to Developers") that allows unstructured information to be recorded.

Author and Date

This section should list when a version of the use case was created and who documented it.

Different templates can have additional sections for suppositions, allowances, recommendations, technical requirements, etc.

Basic Course of Events

At a minimum, each use case should convey a primary scenario, or the typical course of events. The main basic course of events is often conveyed as a set of usually numbered steps, for example:

1. The system prompts the user to enter his account information.
2. The user enters their account number and password.
3. The system validates the login information.
4. The system enters user on to system.

Use Cases and the Development Process

The precise way use cases are used with a given development process depends on which development methodology is being used. Sometimes, a brief use case survey is all that is required. In other development methodologies, the use cases progress in complexity and change in character as the development process proceeds. In some development situations, they begin as brief business use cases, evolve into more detailed system use cases, and then eventually develop into highly detailed and exhaustive test cases.

Benefits of Use Cases

In the earlier days of developing software systems, copious notes were taken and placed in huge documents. Use cases are a nimbler format for capturing what a learning environment's software is required to do.

Use cases have several advantages:

- Use cases are reusable. They can vary at each iteration from a method of capturing requirements to software development recommendations to an experimental case and finally into user documentation.
- When employing different routes, use cases acquire supplementary behaviors that can improve the system's resilience.
- Since use cases are flexible and resilient, they are useful for scoping. They can be relatively easily added and removed from a software project as priorities change.
- Use cases use language that is familiar to users so they understand them. Therefore, use cases are excellent conduits between developers and users.
- Use case specifications can be written in a variety of styles to suit the needs of the project.
- Use cases allow us to tell stories. It is very easy to describe a use case in a concrete way by turning it into a story or scenario.
- Use cases are concerned with the interactions between the user and the system. They tell the story of how the system will behave and what the user can expect.

Limitations of Use Cases

Use cases are not without their limitations:

- Use cases templates do not automatically ensure clarity. Clarity depends on the skill of the writer(s).
- Use cases have a learning curve involved in interpreting them correctly, for both end users and programmers.
- Use case developers often find it difficult to determine the level of user interface (UI) dependency to incorporate in the use case. While use case theory suggests

that UI not be reflected in use cases, many find it awkward to abstract out this aspect of design as it makes the use cases difficult to visualize.

- Use cases say little about the data required for the tasks.
- Use cases cope poorly with non-task activities (activities that are not real work tasks, but where product functionality is still required). For example, ad hoc reports, games, browsing without a precise goal, and various supervisory functions (e.g. checking the system itself is working smoothly).

Reference

Cockburn, A. (2000). *Writing effective use cases* (1st ed., paperback). Addison-Wesley Professional. ISBN 0-201-70225-8.

Chapter 2
IPO Diagrams

Types

The VTOC diagram (also called a hierarchy diagram) can be very useful to the designer. It is extremely easy to draw and the diagram lends itself to group construction and thus is a valuable aid when several people must participate as a team.

Also, the diagram is important in structuring and documenting that participation. Even when the "group" is composed of only the designer and one other person, the designer may want to use the diagram to structure the interview. Finally, the diagram is useful for making presentations at various levels of detail, depending on the intended audience because it can clearly illustrate the hierarchical relationships among various functions and potions of the environments. Finally, the VTOC diagram can also provide a basis for continuous and evolving documentation and contribute greatly to overall project control. Figure 2.1 depicts a possible VTOC diagram for the tuition calculation process.

The advantage of IPO is that it permits a more extended description of processes in ordinary English than a VTOC diagram does. Also, it describes a system at its most basic components: inputs, processes and outputs that are related in an organized manner (Curry et al. 2006). Thus, the processing steps may be briefly described in the process box and more fully explained in the extended description notes at the bottom of the IPO form. The symbols that describe inputs and outputs resemble standard flowcharting symbols. There are, however, possible drawbacks in this reliance on verbal description and flowchart-like drawings; specifically, the documentation time required to describe all the functions may be very high. This drawback has led some designers to use a mixture of diagramming techniques together with

© Association for Educational Communications and Technology (AECT) 2018
J. Frantiska, Jr., *Visualization Tools for Learning Environment Development*,
SpringerBriefs in Educational Communications and Technology,
https://doi.org/10.1007/978-3-319-67440-7_2

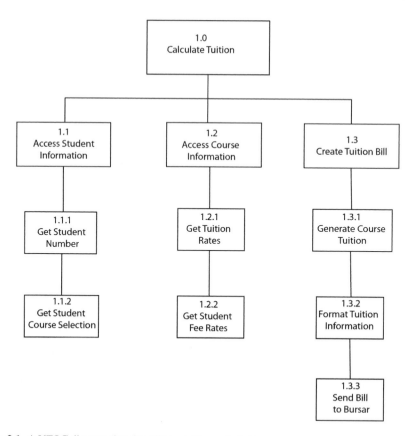

Fig. 2.1 A VTOC diagram that describes a tuition calculation process

the VTOC aspect of IPO. These designers use IPO diagramming only when its extended-description advantages are judged to be worth the added documentation effort. Figure 2.2 describes an IPO diagram to calculate tuition in the university example.

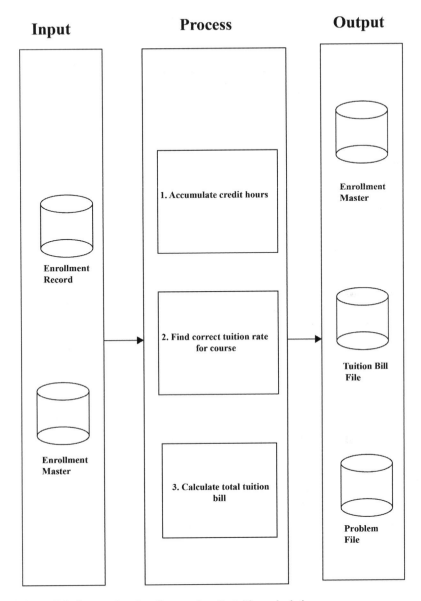

Fig. 2.2 An IPO diagram that describes a university tuition calculation process

Reference

Curry, A., Flett, P., & Hollingsworth, I. (2006). *Managing information and systems: The business perspective*. New York: Routledge.

Chapter 3
Flowcharts

Flowchart Development Tools

What tools can be used to develop flowcharts? A low-tech approach involves buying a flowcharting template (Fig. 3.1) from a retailer such as Staples. There are numerous types of templates with differing symbols and layouts for various purposes.

Flowcharting templates can provide functionality for a diverse range of applications (Fig. 3.2). Flowcharts use specific shapes to represent a variety of actions or steps in a process. Lines and arrows delineate the flow of a sequence of steps, and the relationships among them.

A more high-tech approach to flowcharting is using the capabilities in current versions of Microsoft Word. As shown in Fig. 3.3, by selecting the Insert tab and then the Shapes pull-down menu, any of the flowchart symbols in Fig. 3.2 can be selected.

While you can internally verbalize and understand the processing that takes place within your application at a high level, it can become complicated as you try to envision the complete, detailed scenario including possible error conditions (Frantiska 2009).

Benefits and Implementation

Flowcharts aid in visualize processes by via the following benefits:

1. **They provide a pictorial means by which the steps comprising a process can be understood.** Different people can have different perspectives of how a process works. A flowchart's pictorial approach can help giving those people the ability to agree on the sequence of steps. This approach promotes understanding

© Association for Educational Communications and Technology (AECT) 2018
J. Frantiska, Jr., *Visualization Tools for Learning Environment Development*,
SpringerBriefs in Educational Communications and Technology,
https://doi.org/10.1007/978-3-319-67440-7_3

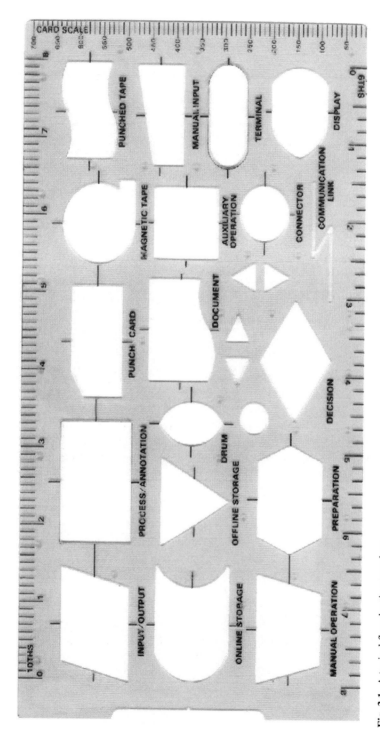

Fig. 3.1 A typical flowcharting template

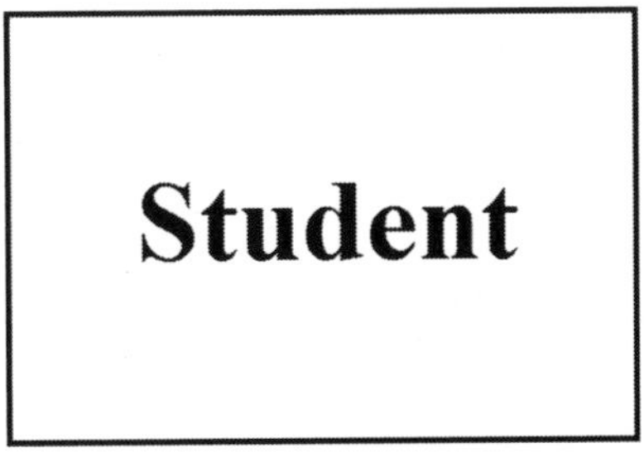

Fig. 3.2 Flowcharting
symbols and their
meanings

Student

where written procedures fail to do so. Just like one picture is worth a thousand words, one flowchart can convey the meaning within many pages of words.

2. **Their standardized format creates a training tool for others.** Due to their highly structured nature, flowcharts aid in training people unfamiliar with the application at hand based upon standardized procedures.
3. **They identify problem areas and opportunities for process improvement.** Once a process is broken down into its steps at the atomic level as diagrams, problem areas become more evident. Opportunities are also highlighted so that the process can be simplified and refined via the analysis of decision points, redundant step s and other areas.

Implementing flowcharts involves the following steps:

1. **Start with the big picture.** It is best to implement flowcharts in a top-down fashion. That is, begin at the most general or macro level and proceed to develop more detailed flowcharts until the system is at its atomic level.
2. **Observe the current process.** For the flowcharts to accurately reflect the process in question, it is necessary to observe the actual process in a detailed manner.
3. **Record the process steps you observed.** As you observe the process steps record them as they occur. For a low-tech approach, record the steps on index cards. If preferred use a software-based approach such as Microsoft Word or Visio. Use different colors to represent each entity involved to help understand and depict the process flow accurately.
4. **Arrange the sequence of steps.** Now arrange the steps exactly as you observed them. Using cards or software allows for the rearrangement of the steps with minimal erasure and redrawing.
5. **Draw the flowchart.** Create the process flow exactly as your final sequence of steps delineates them.

The proper combination of flowchart symbols allows for an application to be communicated via a common language. To understand the basics of flowcharting a basic example of what the symbols represent and how they can be combined will be examined (Frantiska 2009). In Fig. 3.4, we see a flowchart that delineates a simple process.

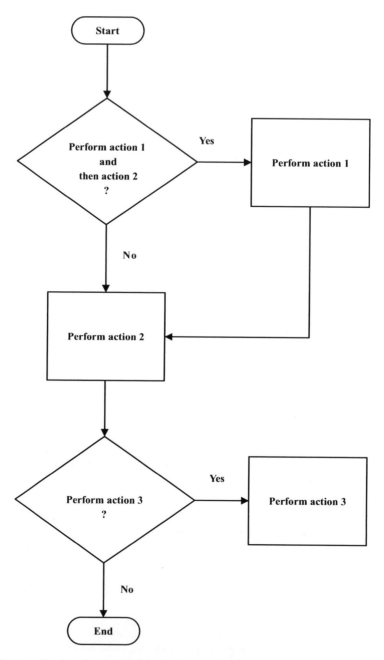

Fig. 3.3 Accessing flowcharting symbols in Microsoft Word

First, create a start/end symbol and label it as "Start". Then draw a line with an arrowhead displaying the direction of the process flow. The actual process is begun by drawing a decision symbol as the endpoint of the process flow line and marking it with the question needed to be answered so that the flow of the process can be determined.

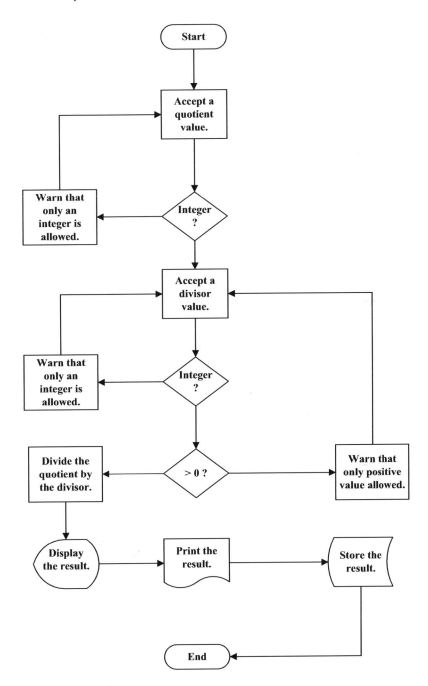

Fig. 3.4 A simple flowchart

For example, if we need to decide if either action 1 will be followed by action 2 or only action 2 be performed, branches coming off the decision symbol with an associated answer (yes or no) are drawn. Therefore, if the answer is "Yes", action 1 will be performed followed by action 2 being performed. Otherwise, if the answer is "No", just action 2 will be performed. The next decision in the process to be encountered is the determination of whether action 3 needs to be performed. A "Yes" answer will cause action 3 to be performed and the program will terminate. A "No" answer will cause the program to terminate with no other processing occurring.

In a more real-world example, a K-12 mathematics teacher wants to employ technology to allow students to develop an instructional application that teaches division.

A student may begin by asking himself "How can I visualize the complexities and interfaces of this application?" It is understood that the process flow of the application can be directed along a number of paths; some can dead-end to errone-ous situations while others can lead to a correct solution. "Measure twice, cut once" definitely applies here as we try to avoid an error situation instead of trying to cor-rect a preventable situation (Frantiska 2009). Doing this requires that we understand what the correct process flow is in addition to potential problem areas and that we develop methods to avoid these areas.

Basic rules of processing and error handling apply to the application portion that performs division. First, the algorithm for this application tentatively accepts the number to be divided (the quotient) and checks to make sure that it is an integer. Second, the number that will divide the quotient (the divisor) is accepted as along as it is also an integer. Additionally, it cannot be zero since zero would create an unde-fined result. Figure 3.5 depicts the steps that describe the flow of control of the application also known as an algorithm which are as follows:

1. Accept a candidate number to be the quotient.
2. Check to see if the candidate quotient is an integer.
3. If not, reject that candidate, display an error message and return to step 1 to accept another quotient candidate.
4. If the quotient is an integer, accept a candidate number to be the divisor.
5. Check to see if the candidate divisor is an integer.
6. If not, apply the processing of step 3 to the candidate divisor.
7. Check to see if the value of the candidate divisor is zero.
8. If it is, reject it, display an error message and return to step 4 to accept another quotient candidate.
9. If it is non-zero, divide the quotient by the divisor.
10. Send the result for display on the user's computer screen.
11. Send the result to the printer to produce a hardcopy.
12. Store the result into a variable for later examination.

While flowcharting allows for insight into the internal processing of an applica-tion, it also provides a means by which the application's functionality can be exam-ined in a clear, succinct fashion to other people who view it as being to some degree arcane. Therefore, the knowledge can be transferred in a structured manner so that other people can apply, improve, and expand the base of information for not only application development but also of the knowledge domains that can be investigated with these applications (Frantiska 2009).

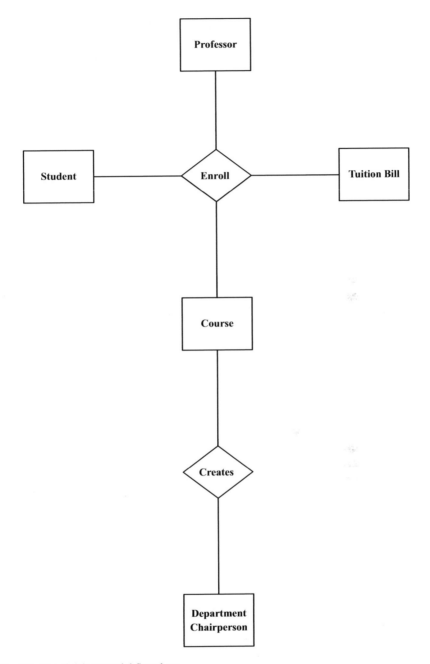

Fig. 3.5 The division tutorial flowchart

Reference

Frantiska, J. J. (2009). Knowing the flow: How flowcharting can help visualize software application development. *ISTE Journal for Computing Teachers-Online*, Spring 2009.

Chapter 4
Entity-Relationship Diagrams

Rationale

Why would we be interested in a data model of a system? Just as the flow of control is an important aspect in the creation of a learning environment, understanding where and how the data is stored is important. What data do we need to use to accomplish various functions within the environment? How are the data related to other data? What function owns the data? What other functions can access the data? As the designer of a learning environment, these questions will apply to you as well since it is up to you to construct the environment so that the data is constructed, accessed, and manipulated so that the expected functionality is realized.

Of course, the notation of the ERD in Fig. 4.1 is quite mysterious at this point. In the following sections, we will examine the structure and components of an ERD; we will then discuss guidelines for drawing a well-structured ERD (Yourdon 1989).

Entity-Relationship Diagram Components

There are three basic elements in ER models:

- Entities are the "things" about which we seek information.
- Attributes are the data we collect about the entities.
- Relationships provide the structure needed to draw information from multiple entities.

These elements are depicted by the following shapes in Fig. 4.2.
In general, a typical ERD looks like the university ERD in Fig. 4.3.
How do we start an ERD?

© Association for Educational Communications and Technology (AECT) 2018
J. Frantiska, Jr., *Visualization Tools for Learning Environment Development*,
SpringerBriefs in Educational Communications and Technology,
https://doi.org/10.1007/978-3-319-67440-7_4

Fig. 4.1 A simple
entity-relationship diagram

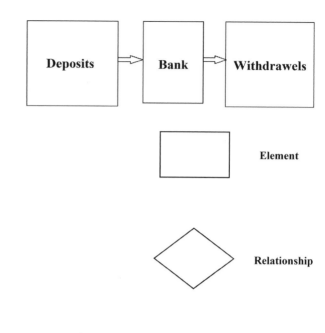

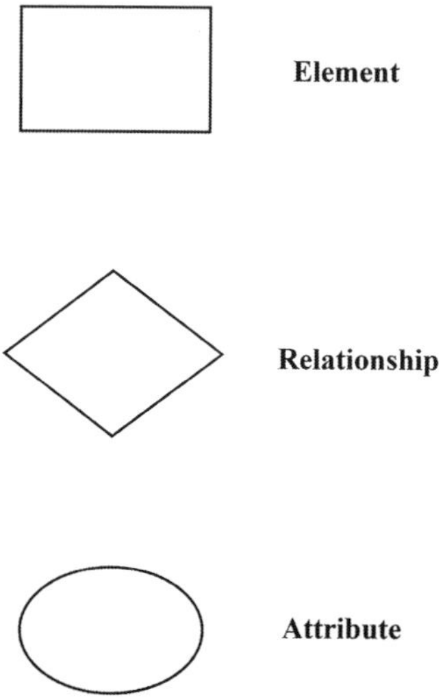

Fig. 4.2 The elements in
an entity relationship
diagram

1. Define Entities: these are usually nouns used in descriptions of the system, in the discussion of business rules, or in documentation; identified in the narrative.
2. Define Relationships: these are usually verbs used in descriptions of the system or in discussion of the business rules (entity _____ entity); identified in the narrative.
3. Add attributes to the relations; the queries determine these, and may also suggest new entities, e.g. grade; or they may suggest the need for keys or identifiers.

    In our university example, what questions can we ask?

- Which professors teach in which classrooms?
- What equipment is in each classroom?
- How many seats are in each classroom?
- What classes are each student enrolled in?

4. Add cardinality (number of elements) to the relations
    That is, there are three types of relationships: one-to-one, one-to-many and many-to-many. For example:
- **One-to-one**: each course has one and only one course number associated with it. So there exists a one-to-one relationship between courses and courses numbers.
- **One-to-many**: each building can contain multiple rooms. So there exists a one-to-many relationship between buildings and rooms.

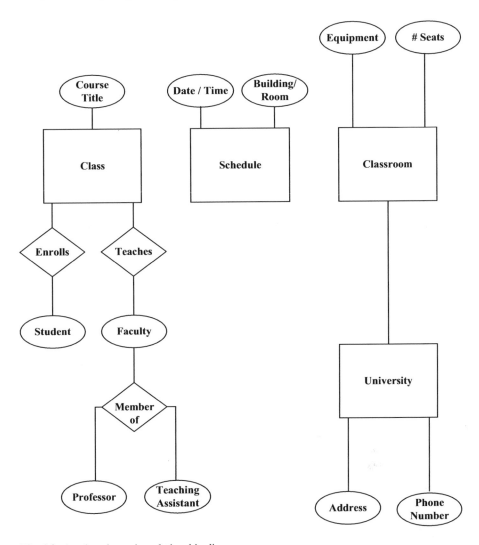

Fig. 4.3 A university entity relationship diagram

- **Many-to-many**: there may be more than one student enrolled in each course, and that each student may be associated with more than one course at a time. So there exists a many-to-many relationship between students and courses.

  There are four major components of an entity-relationship diagram:

1. Entities – the objects whose information we want to model and understand and are of three possible types. For example, **COURSE**. Entities can also be associative or supertype/subtype.
2. Relationships – describe how two or more entities are related to one another. For example, **TEACHES**.
3. Attributes – are the data that describe an entity. Such as **COURSE NUMBER**.

Developing an ERD requires an understanding of the system and its components.

Consider a university:

STUDENTS are taught in a single **COURSE** by the **PROFESSOR** assigned to that **COURSE**. Usually each **STUDENT** will be assigned a single **PROFESSOR**, but in rare cases they may have two.

TEACHING ASSISTANTS also attend to the **STUDENTS;** a number of these are associated with each classroom.

Initially the system will be concerned solely with attendance. Each **STUDENT** is required to take multiple **COURSES** a certain number of times per academic year.

The system must record details concerning **STUDENT** attendance and staff payment. Some staff are paid part time and **PROFESSORS** and **TEACHING ASSISTANTS** work varying amounts of time at varying rates (subject to grade).

The system will also need to track what attendance are required for which **STUDENTS** and when and it should be capable of calculating the cost of class attendance per semester for each **STUDENT**.

Entity Types

An entity type is represented by a rectangular box on an entity-relationship diagram; an example is shown in Fig. 4.4. It represents a collection or set of *objects* (things) in the real world whose individual members (or instances) have the following characteristics:

- *Each can be identified uniquely.* There is some way of differentiating between individual instances of the entity type. For example, if we have an entity type known as **STUDENT**, we must be able to distinguish one student from another (perhaps by last name, or by Social Security number). If all students are the same (if we are operating a business where students are just nameless, faceless blobs who come into our store to buy things), then **STUDENT** would not be a meaningful entity type.
- *Each plays a necessary role in the system.* That is, for the entity type to be valid, it must be a critical part of the system which could not function without it. If we are building an admissions system for our university, it might occur to us that in addition to students, the school has a staff of custodians, each of whom is individually identified by name. While custodians play an important role in the university, the admissions system can function without them; therefore, they do not deserve a role as an entity type in the admissions system model. Obviously, this is something that must be verified with the users as you build your model.
- *Each can be described by one or more data elements.* Thus, a **STUDENT** can be described by such data elements as name, address, social security number, and phone number. Many textbooks describe these as attributing data elements to an entity type. Note that the attributes must apply to each instance of the entity type; for example, each student must have a name, address, social security number, phone number, etc.

Fig. 4.4 An entity type

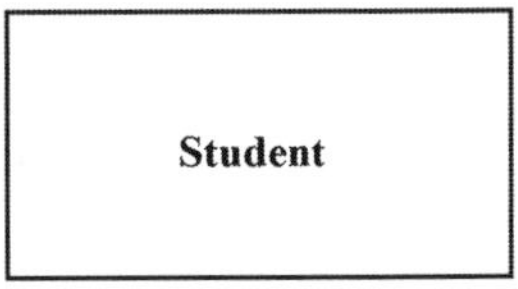

In many systems, entity types will be the system's representation of a corresponding element in the real world. Therefore, entities typically are students, faculty, staff, furniture, and the like. The *entity* is the material thing in the real world, and the *entity type* is the system representation. On the other hand, an entity may also be something nonmaterial such as course schedules, lesson plans, teaching standards, learning strategies, and curriculum maps are but a few examples.

Since people are often entity types in a system, keep something else in mind, too: a person (or, for that matter, any other material thing) could be several different entity types in different data models *or even within the same data model.* John Smith, for example, may be an **EMPLOYEE** in one data model and a **STUDENT** in a different data model; he could also be an **EMPLOYEE** and a **STUDENT** within the same data model.

Relationships

Entities are connected to one another by relationships. A relationship represents a set of connections between entities and is represented by a diamond. Be aware that this diamond is not a logical decision point as is the diamond used to signify a decision in flowcharting diagrams. Figure 4.5 shows a simple relationship that could exist between two or more entities.

It is important to recognize that the relationship represents a set of connections. Each instance of the relationship represents an association between zero or more occurrences of one entity and zero or more occurrences of the other entity. Thus, in Fig. 4.5, the relationship labeled **PASSES** might contain the following individual instances:

- instance 1: student 1 passes quiz 1
- instance 2: student 2 passes quizzes 2 and 3
- instance 3: student 3 passes quiz 4
- instance 4: student 4 passes quizzes 5, 6, and 7
- instance 5: student 5 passes no quizzes
- instance 6: students 6 and 7 passes quiz 8
- instance 7: students 8, 9, and 10 passes quizzes 9, 10, and 11
- etc.

Therefore, a relationship can connect two or more instances of the same entity. Note that the relationship represents something that must be *remembered by* the

Fig. 4.5 A relationship

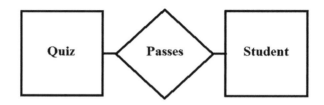

system – something that could not be calculated or derived mechanically. The relationship represents system memory as does an entity.

Note also that there can be more than one relationship between two entities. Figure 4.6, for example, shows two different relationships between a **STUDENT** and a **BURSAR**. Initially, you might think this is emphasizing the obvious: every time the bursar enrolls a student in a course, he invoices the student for the cost of that course. But Fig. 4.7 suggests that the situation might be different: it may turn out, for example, that there are several different instances of a "service" between a bursar and the same student (i.e., an initial service of enrolling the student, other services such as invoicing for courses, etc.). And Fig. 4.6 implies that the invoicing relationship is entirely separate from the enrollment relationship: perhaps some students are invoiced only for their first course, while others are invoiced for every course, and still others are not invoiced at all such as senior citizens in some states can take courses on a space available basis for free.

A more common situation is to see multiple relationships between multiple entities. Figure 4.7 shows the relationship that typically exists between a **STUDENT**, a **BURSAR**, student services and the office of faculty development, for the development, cost, and enrollment in a course.

With a complex diagram like the one in Fig. 4.7 (which is typical of, if not simpler than, the ERDs you are likely to find in a real project), the relationship and its connected entity types should be read as a unit. The relationship can be described from the perspective of *any* of the participating entity types, and all such perspectives are valid. It is the set of all perspectives that completely describes the relationship. For example, in Fig. 4.7, we can read the "discuss cost" relationship in any of the following three ways:

1. Student loan officer discusses the course cost between student and bursar.
2. Student discusses the course cost with the bursar, through student loan officer.
3. Bursar discusses the course cost with the student, through student loan officer.

Note that, in some cases, we can have relationships between different instances of the same entity type. For example, imagine a system being developed for a university, in which **STUDENT, LOAN OFFICER, STUDENT,** and **BURSAR** are entity types. Most of the relationships that we will concentrate on are between instances of different entity types (e.g., the relationships "enrolls in," "teaches," etc.). However, we might need to model the relationship "is a prerequisite for" between one instance of **STUDENT** and another instance of **STUDENT**.

Fig. 4.6 Multiple
relationships between
objects

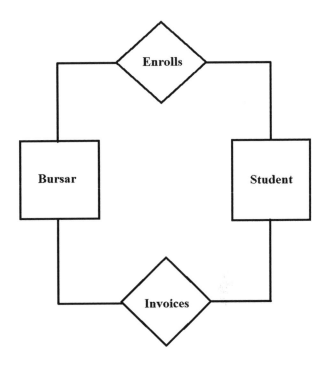

Associative Entities

An *associative entity* is an element of the E-R diagram that can function as both an
entity and a relationship. If there are more than one attributes on a relationship then the
relationship should probably be represented as an entity type. That is, an associative
entity. It associates the instances of one or more entity types and contains attributes
that are specific to the relationship between those entity instances. When the following
four conditions exist, then an entity should be represented as an associative entity:

1. All the relationships are 'many' relationships. For example, the relationship
   ENROLL allows each of many students to enroll in multiple courses.
2. The associative entity has independent meaning to the users, and can preferably
   be recognized with an identifier of a single attribute.
3. The associative entity has one or more attributes in addition to the identifier
   (label).
4. The associative entity is a member of at least one relationship independent of the
   entities related in the associated relationship.

In the case of a student enrolling in a course or courses, it is important to understand that the *relationship* of **ENROLL** sole purpose is to *associate* a **STUDENT**
and *at least* one **COURSE**. What if there is some data that we wish to remember
about each instance of **ENROLL** (e.g., the date of course enrollment)? Where can
this attribute be retained? "Enrollment date" is not an attribute of **STUDENT**, nor
of **COURSE**. Instead, we attribute "enrollment_date" to the **ENROLL** entity and
depict it in a diagram as in Fig. 4.8 (Yourdon 1989).

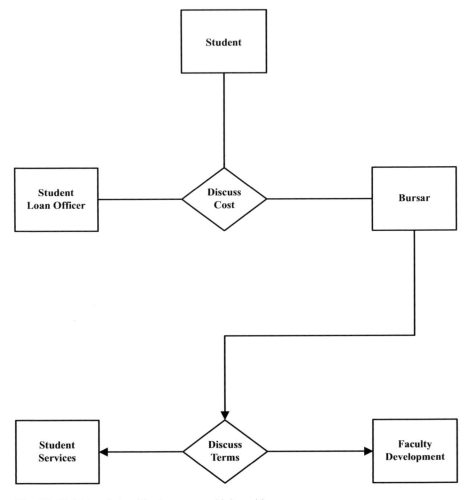

Fig. 4.7 Multiple relationships between multiple entities

ENROLL is now written within a rectangular box and that it is connected with a directed line to an unnamed relationship diamond. This is meant to indicate that **ENROLL** functions as:

An entity type which has information to be stored. In the enrollment example, it is desired to store the date when the enrollment occurred along with the course connected to the student.

A relationship connecting the two entity types of **STUDENT** and **COURSE**. The important aspect here is that **STUDENT** and **COURSE** stand on their own. These would exist whether or not there was an **ENROLL** relationship. Conversely, **ENROLL** obviously owes its very existence on the **STUDENT** and the **COURSE**. It comes into existence only as the result of a relationship between the other entities to which it is connected.

The relationship in Fig. 4.8 is deliberately unnamed. This is because the associative entity name (**ENROLL**) is also the name of the relationship.

Fig. 4.8 An associative entity type

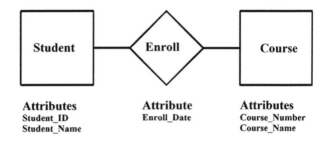

Attributes
Student_ID
Student_Name

Attribute
Enroll_Date

Attributes
Course_Number
Course_Name

Fig. 4.9 A supertype/subtype indicator

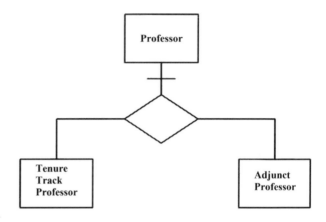

Supertype/Subtype Entity

Finally, we will look at the supertype/subtype entity which consists of an entity type and one or more subtypes, connected by a relationship. Figure 4.9 depicts a representative supertype/subtype where the supertype is **PROFESSOR** and the subtypes are **TENURE TRACK PROFESSOR** and **ADJUNCT PROFESSOR**. An important aspect is that the subtypes are linked to the parent supertype by way of an unnamed relationship. Also note that the symbol that connects supertype and the relationship is a line with a crossbar through it.

In this notation, the supertype is defined by the data elements that apply to *all* subtypes. In Fig. 4.9 for example, all **PROFESSOR**s can be described by such attributes as:

Name
Department
Home address
Department_Chairperson

However, different attributes describe each subtype; otherwise, there would be no reason to distinguish between them. For example, we could imagine that a **TENURE TRACK PROFESSOR** is described by such attributes as:

Annual_salary
Annual_benefits
Tenure_review_date

The **ADJUNCT PROFESSOR** entity might be described by such attributes as:

Salary_per_course
Adjunct_benefits
Adjunct_start_date

Reference

Yourdon, E. (1989). *Modern structured analysis*. Englewood Cliffs: Yourdon Press/Prentice-Hall.

Chapter 5
Information Mapping

In 1965, Robert E Horn, a psychologist at Columbia University, conducted research on how readers deal with large amounts of complex information. His research, roughly based on Learning Theory and Cognitive Psychology, resulted in a standard approach for organizing and communicating information, referred to by the name Information Mapping.

Block Paradigm

Information Mapping™ is a set of principles and procedures that break apart complex information into its atomic elements and then present those elements in an optimal way for the reader so that they can quickly and easily scan and retrieve the information they need. The central aspect in Information Mapping™ is the information block (Horn 1989). Horn realized during his research was that the paragraph is too vaguely defined to be a solid unit of information, and he replaced it by the block.

A **block** is a chunk of information organized around a single subject containing one clear purpose. Refer to the discussion of chunks and chunking in Chap. 2.

A block is composed of one or more sentences, formulas, or figures, and is always identified by a clear label or title. Typically, a block has no more than nine sentences.

The next higher level of information is the map, which is a collection of one to nine blocks all related to a specific topic. Several related maps can be joined to build a document. Documents, maps, and blocks are all regarded as components. And blocks are the smallest reusable components to be managed.

© Association for Educational Communications and Technology (AECT) 2018   31
J. Frantiska, Jr., *Visualization Tools for Learning Environment Development*,
SpringerBriefs in Educational Communications and Technology,
https://doi.org/10.1007/978-3-319-67440-7_5

Horn's Seven Principles for Structuring Information

Information Mapping™ consists of a set of seven principles to organize information effectively so that it is easy to access, understand, and remember. It relies on George Miller's aforementioned magical number seven plus or minus two principle.

1. Chunking
   Chunk or group content into small "bite size" manageable units to make information more accessible for memorization or comprehension. For example, when decomposing information about farming, group all plowing information together, all plantings information together and all irrigation information together.
2. Relevance
   The grouped information must be related to one another with no irrelevant information included. For example, with the plowing information do not information about how to buy a pickup truck to be included.
3. Labelling
   Give a meaningful label or title to each chunk; labels show organization such as "Plowing_ Equipment".
4. Consistency
   Use the same labels, titles, formats and/or structures for the same subjects
5. Integrated graphics
   Use illustrations, figures, and tables so that they complement and clarify the associated text.
6. Accessible detail
   Use details, illustrations, and/or clarifications where needed to provide any abstract presentations with concrete examples.
7. Hierarchy of chunking and labelling
   Organize an accessible structure for content chunks by grouping them into larger chunks and labeling them. Chunks without a hierarchy and label are difficult to find and understand. As in our farming example, at the highest level we might have "Farming" followed at the next level of detail with "Plowing", "Planting" and "Irrigation". Each of those sections would have to be decomposed at the next level. For example, "Irrigation" might contain "Reservoirs", Piping and "Water Trucks".

One criticism of the Information Mapping method is that some writers, especially experienced one may find it somewhat restrictive of their usual degree of creativity. Analyze the subject matter and categorize it based on the specific purpose for a given audience. Using the Information Mapping™ approach, all information can be captured into seven information types as shown in Fig. 5.1.

Example
Before: An Emergency Medical Procedure
   How to perform Cardio Pulmonary Resuscitation

1. Check for response (Hello, hello, are you okay?, tap on shoulder, etc.) Wait for response for 5 s; No response.
2. Look for signs of breathing (chest rise / fall, face movements, etc.)

Information Type	Description
Procedure	A sequence of steps that must be performed to obtain a specified result or outcome.
Process	A sequence of events that occur with an identifiable purpose or result.
Structure	An object that can be divided into separate portions.
Concept	A group of items all of which possess a common set of attributes unique to the group. The items can all be referred to by the same generic name or symbol.
Principle	A statement that expresses what should or should not be done. A rule of action.
Fact	Something known to exist or to have happened based on actual experience or observation.
Classification	Sorting of chunks into categories or classes.

Fig. 5.1 Information mapping's seven types of information

3. Check for pulse for 5 to 10 s. If there is no pulse absent, start CPR. (4 cycles of 15 chest compressions and 2 mouth-to-mouth breaths.)
4. Call for help. (Help! Dial 911!)
5. Locate landmark for chest compression.
6. Demonstrate correct technique of compression. (compress at least 2 inches, say mnemonic ("one and two and ...")
7. Assess pulse and breathing after 5 cycles (about 2 min)
8. If breathing is absent but pulse is present, perform rescue breathing
    - Give 12 rescue breaths in 1 min
9. Assess airway.
10. Check airway (tongue-jaw lift, remove foreign body if visible)
11. Open airway (head tilt-chin lift or jaw thrust)
12. Check breathing (look, listen, feel) up to 10 s
13. Give 1st quick breath (2 sec/breath) & watch chest rise
14. Turn victim to recovery position. Check for pulse and breathing at every 5 min interval.

After: The Information Mapping Version

How to Perform Cardio Pulmonary Resuscitation

Introduction You must complete these procedures to perform Cardio Pulmonary Resuscitation.

- Responsiveness assessment.
- Chest compressions.
- Mouth-to-mouth respiration.

Assessment of Responsiveness Procedure

Step	Action
1.	Establish unresponsiveness – Call, tap or shake the victim
2.	Look for signs of breathing (chest rise / fall, movement of face, etc.)
3.	Check carotid pulse – Locate landmark & palpate up to 10 s – If no pulse, start CPR
4.	Call for help or dial 911

Chest Compression Procedure

Step	Action
5.	Locate landmark for chest compression
6.	Demonstrate correct technique of compression – Correct body and hand position – Compress vertically at least 2 inches downward – Say mnemonic (1 & 2 & 3 & 4 & 5...) – Give cycle of 15 chest compressions and 2 mouth-to-mouth breaths. – Go to step 11
7.	Assess pulse and breathing after 5 cycles (about 2 min)
8.	If breathing is absent but pulse is present, perform rescue breathing – Give 12 rescue breaths in 1 min
9.	Assess pulse then breathing again. (All present)
10.	Place the victim in the recovery position when: – Victim is unconscious – There is no evidence of trauma – Spontaneous breathing present – Successfully resuscitated with the presence of pulse and breathing

Mouth-to-Mouth Respiration Procedure

Step	Action
11.	Assess airway – Check airway (tongue-jaw lift, remove foreign body if visible) – Open airway (head tilt-chin lift or jaw thrust) – Check breathing (look, listen, feel) up to 10 s – Give first quick breath (2 sec/breath) & watch chest rise
12.	If Suspect Choking – Chest does not rise (re-tilt head and give another quick breath) – Chest still does not rise (confirm choking) – Go to step 6.
13.	Unconscious Choking – Locate landmark for chest compression with correct body and hand position – Compress vertically 4–5 cm downwards – Say mnemonic (1 & 2 & 3 & 4 & 5...) – 15 compressions and tongue-jaw lifts until foreign bodies seen and remove it

Reference

Horn, R. E. (1989). *Mapping hypertext: The analysis, organization, and display of knowledge for the next generation of on-line text and graphics.* Lexington: Lexington Institute.

Chapter 6
Learning Objects

A Standard Definition

To bring about a standardized definition of learning objects so that there would exist a commonality of function to promote widespread usage, the Learning Technology Standards Committee (LTSC) of the Institute of Electrical and Electronics Engineers (IEEE) was formed in 1996 to develop and promote instructional technology standards (LTSC 2000a, b). The term Learning Object was first popularized by Wayne Hodgins in 1994 when he named the Computer Education Management Association working group "Learning Architectures, APIs and Learning Objects" was chosen to describe these small instructional components (Wiley 2000). The working group provided the following working definition:

> Learning Objects are defined here as any entity, digital or non-digital, which can be used, re-used or referenced during technology supported learning. Examples of technology-supported learning include computer-based training systems, interactive learning environments, intelligent computer-aided instruction systems, distance learning systems, and collaborative learning environments. Examples of Learning Objects include multimedia content, instructional content, learning objectives, instructional software and software tools, and persons, organizations, or events referenced during technology supported learning.
>
> The following principles about learning objects were developed:

1. They are self-contained as each learning object can be used independently.
2. They are reusable in that a single learning object may be used in multiple contexts for multiple purposes.
3. They can be grouped into larger collections of content, including traditional course structures.
4. Every learning object has descriptive information called metadata which allows it to be easily found by a search.

Does anybody really use or care about learning objects? Learning objects have had considerable impact on an international basis. As with any new concept there can be some ambiguity in its usage and understanding, but it generally pertains to small, reusable units of learning (Polsani 2003; Campbell 2003). The conventional approach

© Association for Educational Communications and Technology (AECT) 2018

J. Frantiska, Jr., *Visualization Tools for Learning Environment Development*, SpringerBriefs in Educational Communications and Technology, https://doi.org/10.1007/978-3-319-67440-7_6

is to regard learning objects as reusable chunks of *content*. Via a building block approach, these learning objects may then be incorporated into higher order learning designs. Pedagogically, the purpose of contexts is to enable learners to achieve learning objectives. The design of these contexts requires choices in the selection and organization of activity and content to assist the learning process (Boyle 2006).

Three main design standards have been used to create learning objects that adhere to the four previously mentioned standards. The first two standards resulted from computer programming, another field that is concerned with building complex structures (programs) from smaller pieces or modules of computer code functionality (Boyle and Cook 2001).

The first standard is that of cohesion. In computer programming, cohesion is a measure of how strongly-related and focused the various responsibilities of a software module are. In the context of learning objects, this standard states that each unit should be dedicated to doing only one function. Each learning object should be based around one clear learning goal or objective. As each unit is self-contained, this should give designers considerable flexibility in how these are selected and used. Again, this is a "building block" approach, that is, the usage of self-contained, dedicated units can be configured into many configurations.

The second structuring standard is that of coupling. In computer programming, coupling which is sometimes referred to as dependency is the degree to which each module relies on other modules within a program. Therefore, it is the exact opposite quality of cohesion which emphasizes module independence.

If a unit is very reliant on other units then it is not independently reusable and violates the basic definition of a learning object. There are two ways in which coupling can be controlled. The first way is that of navigational bindings which are relations amongst modules of pieces of software based upon how the navigation of a website is structured. The navigation structure dictates what modules invoke or are invoked by other modules. There should be no *necessary* navigational bindings to other units. The classic hypertext method of instruction with numerous embedded links is thus a poor example for learning objects. The second way of coupling control is context bindings which dictate how the content of modules makes them dependent upon one another. The content of the object should not refer to and be dependent on content in other objects. (Bradley and Boyle 2004)

These two structuring standards facilitate the design of independent, reusable learning objects. However, there is a potential danger that such self-contained objects might constrain the richness of the learning experience. Therefore, a third structuring standard was introduced to enable the generation of rich learning experiences from cohesive, self-contained objects – compound objects. A compound object consists of two or more independent objects that are linked to create the compound. This compound consists of a base object and optional expansions. For example, the base object could be a text-based webpage that focuses on one topic, say an explanation of aerodynamics in Java. This can operate as an independent learning object. All the links to the optional objects are placed in a separate column on the right-hand side of the page.

As previously discussed, there are numerous definitions of what a learning object is. An additional problem is that many of the definitions are very broad and sometimes all encompassing. The LTSC defines them as "any entity, digital or non-digital, which can be used, re-used or referenced during technology supported learning". Another definition is from (McGee and Katz 2005) that views learning objects as "any digital resource that is designed to support learning, and may be re-used in different learning contexts (traditional or informal) for different purposes. We do not exclude technical data objects or information objects but rather see a division between these and those designed specifically to support *learning*."

With such broad definitions, the definition of a learning object is still rather nebulous. Videotapes, web sites, audio tapes, software, etc. are designed with a single target audience, one instructional objective, and one learning context in mind.

However, learning objects are designed with change in mind: change of content, change in access, and change of target audience. This requires that designers and instructors understand the concept of a learning object life cycle that describes the linear process of birth, use, and death of an object. The learning object life cycle is dynamic and iterative, and evolves over time and in relation to the context in which they are used. In fact, the learning object life cycle is comprised of birth, use, *re-use* and death of an object.

The learning object description in Fig. 6.1 covers a Forces of Flight learning object in a module called Science. In this context, a learning object equates to a lesson.

A common metaphor used to explain assets and objects is Lego blocks. Content assets can be snapped together with a practice asset and some assessment assets to create a learning object. Learning objects can be snapped together to create lessons and modules. Again, a main aspect of a learning object is that it can, will and should be re-used in various situations (Herridge Group 2002).

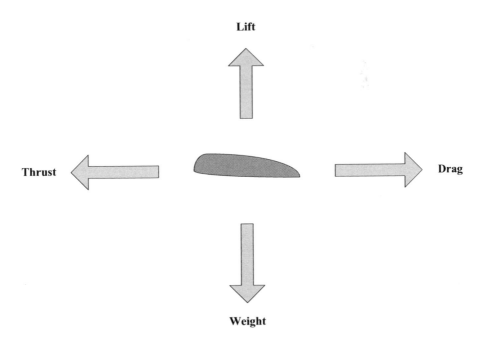

Fig. 6.1 A learning object description

Types

There are many different types of learning objects with each serving a different purpose. Dr. David A. Wiley an Associate Professor of Instructional Psychology & Technology at Brigham Young University created a taxonomy of learning objects. Developed in 2000, it was called "Preliminary Taxonomy of Learning Object Types". In this taxonomy, he developed five types of learning objects listed below with an example of each:

- *Fundamental* – A learning object that is at its most basic level so that it cannot be broken down any further. For example: a diagram of sub-atomic particles.
- *Combined-closed* – A learning object that contains at least two Fundamental type learning objects that are connected so that the Fundamental objects can't be reused with any other objects. For example: an animation of the Wright brother's first flight with accompanying audio narration.
- *Combined-open* – A learning object that contains at least two Fundamental learning objects connected so that reuse of the Fundamentals is possible. For example, a web page dynamically connecting the previously mentioned animation and narration files with textual material "on the fly."
- *Generative-presentation* – A learning object that combines or generates and then combines combined-closed and fundamental type learning objects. For example, a multimedia-based program that generates the Wright brothers animation and narration files and places them to present a flight scenario to the learner.
- *Generative-instructional* – A learning object that combines fundamental, combined-closed types, and generative-presentation learning objects and then evaluates how the learner interacts with them. For example, a website that instructs the learner to successively add the necessary steps in the proper sequence to create the Wright brother's first flight. It uses instructions such as "recollect and narrate a series of steps that allow the Wright brothers to fly".

In 2003, Clive Shepherd, chairman of the eLearning Network developed the Learning Object Design Assistant or LODA. LODA is a job aid that helps instructional designers in creating effective, flexible materials that support e-learning performance.

LODA defines a learning object as "A learning object is a small, reusable digital component that can be selectively applied – alone or in combination – by computer software, learning facilitators or learners themselves, to meet individual needs for learning or performance support" (Shepherd and Kori 2003).

LODA facilitates the selection of 41 object types. Some are self-contained whereas others are used as modules in larger structures for learning or performance support. They are comprised of three object categories:

Tutorials – Brief, self-contained chunks of learning, in any area of knowledge, skill, or attitude. Include information, practice activities and all other elements necessary for effective learning.

Tutorial Types

Facts and Background Information Important facts that need to be remembered or information to support other tutorial types. Use this object type when the validity of the information is independent of any other information or when to integrate the information directly into other types of tutorial might risk cognitive overload for the learner.

Concepts/Classes Distinctions between classes (types) of objects, events, people or ideas and their unique attributes. Examples: perspectives in politics; types of computers; the concept of equality; the concept of object-orientation. Use this object type when the validity of the information is independent of any other information or when to integrate the information directly into other types of tutorial might risk cognitive overload for the learner.

Structure The configuration of an object or environment. Examples: the parts of an airplane; a corporate organization diagram; the blueprint of a building; the components of a software interface. Use this object type when the validity of the information is independent of any other information or when to integrate the information directly into other types of tutorial might risk cognitive overload for the learner.

Rule What to do in specific situations, i.e. "if ... then do ...". Examples: never ask a question unless you know the answer; do not use the office phone for personal calls; teach arithmetic before calculus; if it starts to smoke, send an alarm. Use this object type when the validity of the information is independent of any other information or when to integrate the information directly into other types of tutorial might risk cognitive overload for the learner.

Principle A generalized assertion, e.g. a law, theory, value, or belief. Examples: the law of gravity; customers are always right. Use this object type when the validity of the information is independent of any other information or when to integrate the information directly into other types of tutorial might risk cognitive overload for the learner.

Attitude An inclination to think, feel or act in a definite way relative to events, people, ideas, etc. Examples: attitudes about the Internet, clients, public speaking, politics, the opposite sex. Use this object type when the validity of the information is independent of any other information or when to integrate the information directly into other types of tutorial might risk cognitive overload for the learner.

Process How something works. A series of events culminating in an object's function. Examples: how a mobile phone works; the object life cycle; the recruitment process; the process by which politicians are elected.

Procedure How to do something. A sequence of steps to accomplish a task. Examples: setting up a website; handling a situation; troubleshooting; filling out a form.

Information Objects Reference materials for performance support or as components in learning strategies requiring multiple learning objects. Examples: procedures; case histories; introductions and summaries; decision aids.

Information Object Types

Facts and Background Information Important facts that need to be remembered or information to support other tutorial types. Use this object type when the validity of the information is independent of any other information or when to integrate the information directly into other types of tutorial might risk cognitive overload for the learner.

Concepts/Classes Differences between object types, actions, individuals or ideas and their unique characteristics. Examples: political attitudes; kinds of processer; the perception of fairness; the notion of object-oriented development. Use this object type when the validity of the information is independent of any other information or when to integrate the information directly into other types of tutorial might risk cognitive overload for the learner.

Structure The arrangement of an object or environment. Examples: the parts of an automobile; an organizational diagram; the blueprint of an airplane part; the parts of a learner-software interface. Use this object type when the validity of the information is independent of any other information or when to integrate the information directly into other types of tutorial might risk cognitive overload for the learner.

Rule What is required to be done in a given situation, i.e. "if ... then do ...". Examples: walk only when the light is green; do not use negative examples; teach reading before writing; if you see fire, sound an alarm. Use this object type when the validity of the information is independent of any other information or when to integrate the information directly into other types of tutorial might risk cognitive overload for the learner.

Principle A sweeping claim, e.g. a rule, concept, value, or confidence. Examples: honesty is the best policy; the customer is always right. Use this object type when the validity of the information is independent of any other information or when to integrate the information directly into other types of tutorial might risk cognitive overload for the learner.

Attitude A disposition to contemplate, sense or perform in a certain way in relation to specific events, persons, concepts, etc. Examples: attitudes about politics, work, speechmaking, government, the opposite sex. Use this object type when the validity of the information is independent of any other information or when to integrate the information directly into other types of tutorial might risk cognitive overload for the learner.

Process How an item works. A sequence of actions that culminate in the expected outcome. Examples: how a cell phone functions; the life cycle of a chicken; the staffing process; the political election process.

Procedure How to perform a task. A arrangement of phases to do something. Examples: installing educational software; rowing a boat; writing a letter.

Decision Aid A tool to help someone to reach an appropriate decision in a specific situation. Examples are flowcharts, expert systems. Uses: judging a college application; selecting a discussion method; choosing a suitable mortgage.

Definition An explanation of the meaning of a term used within one or more other learning objects.

Demonstration/Worked Example An implementation of the steps that make up a procedure. Examples: a multimedia-based demonstration of how to make a presentation; a written example of how to build a boat. Use this object type when to include the demonstration directly within a procedure could cause cognitive overload for the learner or when tailored demonstrations are required for different audiences.

Illustration/Story/Case history A method to demonstrate how a process, procedure or rules can be applied in a specific situation. Examples: medical review; news articles describing disasters; an anecdote describing how an invention can be adapted for specific tasks. Use this object type when to include the material directly within another tutorial or information object could cause cognitive overload for the learner or when tailored illustrations are required for different target audiences.

Paper A source of reference to support any type of learning or work activity. Examples: a research report; a summary of the competition in a market; a review of alternative theories; a detailed proposal.

Program introduction The initial component in a learning strategy involving multiple learning objects. Necessary to ensure the suitability or motivation of the program to the learner.

Program Conclusion The final component in a learning strategy involving multiple learning objects. Necessary to integrate and summarize the material and to encourage transfer of learning.

Practice Objects Practice, assessment, and discovery-learning activities for use within learning strategies requiring multiple learning objects. Examples: scenarios; tests; simulations.

Offline Procedural Practice An activity that offers an opportunity to practice a procedure not requiring direct interaction with the learning object. Examples: using a software application for a specific task; a rehearsing a play; assembling parts; combining chemicals to produce a paint. Use this object type when the procedure cannot effectively be practiced online, or when to include the practice directly within a procedure tutorial would cause cognitive overload for the learner, or when tailored practice activities are required for different target audiences.

Case Study/Scenario/Problem An activity in which the learner is presented with a specific situation and is required to reply to that situation in a specific way. Examples: a moot court case study, investigating a crime; reviewing a video of a criminal cross-examination; a statement of profits and losses for a company. Use this object type when to include the scenario directly within a tutorial could cause cognitive overload for the learner or when tailored scenarios are required for different target audiences or different levels within an audience.

Simulation A representation of one or more real-life processes, in which the user can initiate action or respond to situations or events. Examples: a flight simulator; a model of corporate governance in which learners can see the effect of their decisions. Use this object type when to include the simulation directly within a tutorial could cause cognitive overload for the learner or when tailored simulations are required for different target audiences.

Game An activity with a goal and rules, in which the learner competes against real or imaginary opponents to improve their ability. Used variously to influence attitudes, or to provide practice or assess proficiency in many types of learning situations, including the recall or recognition of facts, applying rules or theories, locating parts or places, or the application of a psychomotor skill. Examples: a business game; a video game to help teach typing; a timed quiz played against the clock. Use this object type when to include the game directly within a tutorial could cause cognitive overload for the learner or when customized games are required for different target audiences.

Drill and Practice An activity designed to increase proficiency in a task, through repeated practice. Used in many types of learning situations, including the recall or recognition of facts, applying rules or theories, locating parts or places, or the application of a psychomotor skill. Examples are a series of sentences to remember and recall; a sequence of computer program structures to identify. Use this object type when to include the practice directly within a tutorial could cause cognitive overload for the learner or when customized practice is required for different target audiences.

Test An activity, typically a series of questions, designed to assess proficiency against specific learning objectives. Examples are a series of short essay questions, submitted to for review; a test composed of a variety of interactive question formats. Use this object type when to include the test directly within a tutorial could cause cognitive overload for the learner or when customized tests are required for different target audiences.

Questionnaire/Inventory A series of questions whose answers the answers when interpreted, provide understanding into a learner's attitudes, personality, preferences, etc. Examples are a questionnaire designed to assess attitudes towards people; a learning style questionnaire; a political opinion poll. Use this object type when to include the questionnaire directly within a tutorial could cause cognitive overload for the learner or when customized questionnaires are required for different target audiences.

Metadata

Merriam-Webster's Online Dictionary defines metadata as "data that provides information about other data" (metadata 2014). Locating a learning object may be accomplished through searching the Internet or a repository, but nothing can be systematically located for use or re-use without metadata. Or-Bach (2004) describes three types of metadata: descriptive, administrative, and structural. Administrative metadata manages and preserves objects in the repository by detailing information such as format, copyrighting, and licensing; structural metadata stores objects in a repository and for presentation by linking objects together to make up logical units; descriptive metadata describes the intellectual content of objects. The purpose of learning object metadata is to provide a common nomenclature enabling learning resources to be described in a common way. Metadata can be collected in catalogs, as well as directly packaged with the learning resource it describes. Metadata has become a critical and well-articulated sub-field of learning objects as noted by the proliferation of different taxonomies.

Learning objects enter the development process depending upon the type of organization and specific need. Higher education has used the development process to help faculty members think deeply about course objectives and instructional design; whereas, the military, government, and corporate sectors implement the development process to create eLearning solutions. Identifying the most appropriate instructional model during the analysis and design phases is critical for the development of effective instruction since it ensures that learning outcomes are directly linked to the learning objectives. For example, let's say that a teacher develops training on how hurricanes form. First, analysis has been conducted and results have identified that the target audience's learning level varies widely. To satisfy all the levels, the teacher will use one or more taxonomies (i.e., Bloom's, etc.) employing variant levels of the chosen taxonomy(s).

In situations where highly specialized content is required due to the target audience's needs, objects will be required to be designed so that the instruction is both relevant and efficacious to that highly specific need. As a result, these objects might not be necessarily reusable or instructionally efficacious in a different instructional context or target audience. Like pieces of a jigsaw puzzle, objects cannot be chosen from a collection "on the fly", as they are not inherently interchangeable, and if interchangeability is attempted, the results are rarely acceptable. Therefore, a great deal of information must be known about a learning object for it to be used effectively across different instructional contexts and, target audiences. The ability to have significant knowledge about an object requires that the object is associated with the correct metadata. This will allow the developer to properly choose the object that best meets both the needs of the designer as well as the target audience.

Use and Re-use

The use and re-use of learning objects is of course how many users come into the learning object life cycle. Use may be limited to a one-time experience, but inherently learning objects should be used repeatedly by different people and possibly in different ways. Re-use should not only pertain to the re-use of objects, but should also focus on the efficient and effective re-use, re-purpose, and reference (R^3) of objects Katz et al. (2004) defines R^3 as the following:

> *Re-use* is the use of an existing object in a new learning event without any modification to its instructional treatment, context, or content. *Re-purpose* refers to the use of an existing object in a new learning event with modification to its instructional treatment, context, or content. *Reference* is the use of an existing object(s) as an information source or resource for generating ideas for new learning events. For example, if teaching color theory, an object may have relevance for physics, art, culinary arts, or interior design. In this case the content remains the same in each situation of re -use, but the context and possible instructional strategy changes. The object may be re-purposed for different levels of abilities, linguistic or cognitive sophistication, or even depth. Finally, the object may be linked to or embedded in a larger sequence of learning objects.

(Polsani 2003) identified reusability as the major functional requirement of learning objects and suggests that learning objects should be created with a high level of abstraction, as this will provide independence from usage scenarios and the ability of the learning object to join other learning objects in a variety of contexts. He suggested as immediate necessities the commonly accepted, accurate, and functionally effective definition of a learning object and the reengineering of the design and development process of learning objects in a "multidisciplinary and cooperative model of development to create knowledge that is appropriate for the emergent network society."

Evaluation and Selection

Prior to selecting a learning object, the user evaluates the object based upon specific criteria such as maintenance, user interface, and effectiveness. Maintenance involves making sure the object works the way it was designed to and that its content is appropriate in the required context. User interface is important especially considering the potential of re-use across various audiences and contexts. Learning objects may be required to interact with other systems that have incompatible interface designs that hinder viewing and interaction. Also, criterion of the Americans with Disabilities Act accommodations may make the most appealing learning object unusable. Evaluation of effectiveness appears to be the most overlooked aspect of the learning object life cycle. Cisco Systems as well as other for-profit companies, does evaluate effectiveness of training, what Cisco refers to as "impact" but the primary focus is on learning achievement rather than effectiveness of learning object design and operation. All of these factors need to be taken into consideration when evaluating and selecting an appropriate learning object.

(Meister-Emerich 2009) delineates an evaluation process of five steps for selecting learning objects as follows:

1. Identify Learning Outcomes

   Learning outcomes list specifically what a student should be able to do upon completion of a course. Inclusion of learning objects that do not directly align with the course learning outcomes are likely to decrease student performance since the student may have difficulty identifying the essential, or important, content. Clearly stated learning outcomes will help select only relevant learning objects.

2. Evaluate the Accuracy of the Learning Object.

   If a learning object presents inaccurate information, uses a technique that is different from the one recommended in the text, or uses a non-standard technique, students may have difficulty. Generally inaccurate content would eliminate a learning object from further consideration. However, if learning objects related to a specific concept are limited a faculty developer may want to include a learning object that has inaccurate content and have the student find and explain the error in it.

3. Evaluate the Content's Usability.

   Presentation design, interaction usability, and accessibility should be evaluated. Split-attention and redundancy effects are two concepts to consider when evaluating presentation design. Split-attention is when the "learner must divide his attention between the text and the graphic to comprehend the material" (Morrison et al. 2004). The redundancy effect is when information is "in both the illustration and the text" and it "actually increases the cognitive effort to process the information" (Morrison et al. 2004). To reduce these effects, a learning object should integrate the images and the text. Auditory information should supplement the on-screen information, but not duplicate it.

(Nesbit et al. 2002) describes interaction usability as, "ease of navigation, predictability of the user interface, and quality of the interface help features" (Smith and Ragan 2005) categorized events where the student generates learning as generative as opposed to those where the instructor supplies the learning which were termed supplantive. Learning objects that presented information, either in a textual or audio-visual format, were listed as supplantive, since students were to read or watch the information, but were passive in use of it. If the problem required the student to think about what the answer to the entry means or relate it to other concepts, it would be classified as generative. Learning objects where students entered information and then had a chance to modify an answer based on the initial entry were listed as generative. The main factor in selecting between generative or supplantive was the student interaction. When assessing interactivity, Evans and Gibbons (2007) found that "adding interactivity to a computer-based lesson increases the depth of learning or understanding". Thus, when reviewing learning objects ones that are relatively static or where user participation is mostly passive should be rejected if ones where the user is actively involved are available."

4. Estimate Cognitive Level.

Another concern is the cognitive level of the learning object. Using Bloom's taxonomy, identify the taxonomy level that best describes the user activity in the learning object. Learning objects at the knowledge level included those that only present information, or where the user would guess and check to determine an answer, or match information or graphics. To classify a learning object at a higher level, the student would be required to interact with it to demonstrate learning. The designer should determine the appropriate cognitive level for the course.

5. Location

Lesson location identifies if, and or where, in a lesson (introduction, body, conclusion, or assessment) the learning object can be used. Location in a lesson is often subjective. However, the designer should identify where and how the learning objects would be used in the course. If there is an existing learning object that fills the same niche, the faculty should decide which is better.

References

Boyle, T. (2006). The design and development of second generation learning objects. In E. Pearson & P. Bohman (Eds.), *Proceedings of world conference on educational multimedia, hypermedia and telecommunications 2006* (pp. 2–12). Chesapeake: AACE.

Boyle, T., & Cook, J. (2001). Online interactivity: Best practice based on two case-studies. *Association for Learning Technology Journal, 9*(1), 94–102.

Bradley, C., & Boyle, T. (2004). The design, development, and use of multimedia learning objects. *Journal of Educational Multimedia and Hypermedia, 13*(4), 371–389. Norfolk: AACE.

Campbell. (2003). *Interoperability and reusable learning objects. PowerPoint slides from Workshop on "Breaking Boundaries: Innovation in medical education"*. Manchester, UK, February 2003. Available at: http://www.medev.ac.uk/docs/breaking_boundaries/campbell_workshop

Evans, C., & Gibbons, N. J. (2007). The interactivity effect in multimedia learning. *Computers & Education, 49*(4), 1147–1160. https://doi.org/10.1016/j.compedu.2006.01.008.

Herridge Group. (2002). *Learning objects and instructional design.* Retrieved July 12, 2017, from: http://www.herridgegroup.com/pdfs/learning%20objects%20&%20instructional%20design.pdf

Katz, H., Worsham, S., Coleman, S., Murawski, M., & Robbins, C. (2004). Reusable learning object model design and implementation: Lessons learned. In *Proceedings of world conference on e-Learning in corporate, government, healthcare, and higher education 2004* (pp. 2483–2490). Norfolk: AACE.

LTSC. (2000a). *Learning technology standards committee website*, [Online]. Available as of July 12, 2017 at https://ieee-sa.imeetcentral.com/ltsc/

LTSC. (2000b). *IEEE standards board: Project authorization request (PAR) form*, [Online]. Available as of July 12, 2017 at http://grouper.ieee.org/groups/ctl/par2000.html

McGee, P., & Katz, H. (2005). A learning object life cycle. In G. Richards (Ed.), *Proceedings of world conference on e-Learning in corporate, government, healthcare, and higher education 2005* (pp. 1405–1410). Chesapeake: AACE.

Meister-Emerich, K. (2009). Five-step procedure for the selection of learning objects. In T. Bastiaens et al. (Eds.), *Proceedings of world conference on e-Learning in corporate, government, healthcare, and higher education 2009* (pp. 534–538). Chesapeake: AACE.

metadata. 2014. In *Merriam-Webster.com*. Retrieved October 18, 2014, from: http://www.mer-riam-webster.com/dictionary/metadata

Morrison, G. R., Ross, S. M., & Kemp, J. E. (2004). *Designing effective instruction*. Hoboken: Wiley.

Nesbit, J. C., Belfer, K., & Vargo, J. (2002). A convergent participation model for evaluation of learning objects. *Canadian Journal of Learning and Technology, 28*(3), 105–120.

Or-Bach, R. (2004). Learning objects and metadata – From instructional design to a cognitive tool. In L. Cantoni & C. McLoughlin (Eds.), *Proceedings of world conference on educational multimedia, hypermedia, and telecommunications 2004* (pp. 2260–2263). Chesapeake: AACE.

Polsani, P. (2003). Use and abuse of reusable learning objects. *Journal of Digital Information, 3*(4). Retrieved July 12, 2017, from: https://journals.tdl.org/jodi/index.php/jodi/article/view/89/88

Shepherd, C., & Kori, D. (2003). *LODA: Learning object design assistant*. Brighton: Above and Beyond Ltd.

Smith, P. L., & Ragan, T. J. (2005). *Instructional design*. Hoboken: Wiley.

Wiley, D. A. (2000). Connecting learning objects to instructional design theory: A definition, a metaphor, and a taxonomy. In D. A. Wiley (Ed.), *The instructional use of learning objects*. Online Version. Retrieved July 9, 2017, from: http://reusability.org/read/chapters/wiley.doc

Summary/Conclusion

This brief has examined the importance of visualization to the educator who is developing learning environments. Like their engineering counterparts, they have a need to understand the inner operation of their product as much as the outer functionality via the use of various tools. This approach allows the educator / developer to have complete understanding of their project. These tools allow the educator / developer to peer into their project to design and assess its structure and content in a structured manner.

While use case diagrams help to design overall functionality, input-process-output diagrams aid in seeing how inputted information is processed and generated as output. Given this functionality and information flow, flowcharts allow the educator / developer to layout how the individual portions of their software need to perform and interact so that the required functionality is realized. The entity-relationship diagram delineates how the information is stored so that the flow and functionality can be accomplished while information mapping helps to see how the information is structured and related.

Functionality, information flow, processing, information storage, structures and relationships provide the educator / developer with a complete understanding of the learning environment that they are developing. This should provide them with a consistent means of development which in turn should give them confidence in the process and their own ability.

© Association for Educational Communications and Technology (AECT) 2018   51
J. Frantiska, Jr., *Visualization Tools for Learning Environment Development*,
SpringerBriefs in Educational Communications and Technology,
https://doi.org/10.1007/978-3-319-67440-7